D0917058

STRAND PRICE
$ 5.00

PAUL CUMMINS

THE COLLECTED POEMS

Best Wishes,

Paul

Jan. 2021

Other Books by Paul F. Cummins

Biographies
Richard Wilbur. Contemporary Writers in Christian Perspective Series, William B. Eerdmans Publishing Co., Grand Rapids, MI, 1971. *Dachau Song: The Twentieth-Century Odyssey of Herbert Zipper.* Peter Lang Publishing Inc., New York, NY, 1992. [Also translated and published in Beijing, China, and Vienna, Austria.] *Max Raferty: A Study in Simplicity.* Hogarth Press, Newhall, CA. First printing March 1968; second printing July 1968.

Education
For Mortal Stakes: Solutions for Schools and Society. Published simultaneously by Bramble Co., Las Vegas, NV, and Peter Lang Publishing Inc., New York, NY, 1992. [Also translated and published in Tokyo, Japan.]
Proceed with Passion: Engaging Students in Meaningful Education. Red Hen Press, Los Angeles, CA, 2004.
Two Americas / Two Educations: Funding Quality Schools for All Students. Red Hen Press, Los Angeles, CA, 2007.
Confessions of a Headmaster: My Pursuit of Joy and Justice in Education. Red Hen Press, Los Angeles, CA, 2015.
Voice and Verse: Joys and Howtos of Teaching, reading and Writing Poetry. Amazon, 2018

Children's Books
The Misadventures of Thomas Hippopotamus. Blurb, 2011.
All Aboard the Train of Thought. Xlibris Corp., 2012.

Poetry
A Postcard from Bali. Argonne House Press, Washington, D.C., 2002.
Undercover, Finishing Line Press, Georgetown, Kentucky, 2012

Copyright © 2019 Paul Cummins

All rights reserved. No part of this publication may be duplicated or transmitted in any form without prior written consent from the publisher, excepting brief quotes used in reviews. Displaying such material without prior permission is a violation of international copyright laws.

Printed in the United States of America
First Printing, 2019

ISBN: 978-0-9998452-9-5
Library of Congress Control Number: 2018954575

Published by Griffith Moon
Santa Monica, California
www.GriffithMoon.com

PAUL CUMMINS

THE COLLECTED POEMS

1966 - 2017

 Griffith Moon

Dedication

To the five special ladies of my life:
Maryann, Liesl, Julie, Anna, Emily

in Memoriam:
Camille (Mimi) Cummins-Adams
Paul Stedman Cummins
Ruth Wenter Cummins
Michelle Hickey
Kenneth Coogan Adams
Herbert Zipper
Joseph E. Cummins

Acknowledgments

I would like to thank my family and friends whose steadfast support and encouragement of my poetry has inspired a lifetime of work. Over the years I have thanked assistants for whom I remain grateful, and I am most recently indebted to Nancy Bryan, who has helped shepherd this book in countless ways. Mostly it is her wisdom I so appreciate. I would like to acknowledge and praise Helen Bartlett, Kate Capshaw, Katie McGrath, Vicky Schorr, and Mona Simpson for their passionate promotion of poetry in the greater community and for their support and encouragement of my own. I would like to thank Jeffrey Graham and Mona Simpson for the close reading and for helpful editorial suggestions. I would like to especially thank my publisher Griffith Moon and to Kimberly Brooks, for her support and encouragement of so many of my projects and especially my poetry. Finally, I must thank my wife/muse, my family and my select friends who not only inspire me to write but who also continue to reassure me that they appreciate my poetry.

Introduction

In *Under Cover*, his second volume of poems, Paul Cummins extends the scope of *A Postcard from Bali* (2002), writing the most difficult poems of all, poems that express contentment with a life that has achieved purpose, "revering each other, our time together...revering the simple blessings of being,...extending in each mind to the very / limits of mortality with intimations of beyond." Yet to write of contentment without being smug or soporific, and without losing a sense of urgency and edge, poses a challenge both formal and formidable, one that Cummins addresses directly. The contentment he celebrates is complicated but not contaminated by a constant awareness of suffering, of history, and of unavoidable, tacit complicity.

In lyric language inflected by classical tradition and nuanced by jazz and slang idiom, Cummins preserves and articulates artistic responsibility: *maintaining the ability to respond* with deep feeling and intelligence, even to events our culture tends to turn away from, in discomfort, such as the deeply personal moment of a loved one's death—as well as the individual tragedies resulting from political atrocity. Cummins holds such experiences up to the light, with language, as he recounts, for example: "The grave recognition, the eyes / Fixing truth beyond boundaries...Hope flickering like candles in a draft."

In these poems, Cummins shares his love of jazz, of color, of dogs, and of literature. He expresses personal devotions to family and friendship and to erotic love, to those who have passed as well as to those who have survived, and to the natural world, where he observes "the universe of intricacy / that so possessed each spider's destiny."

As he examines memory, Cummins plumbs the depths of gratitude to find the crystalline salt of wisdom, distilling the essential experience and rendering, with evident savor, the pleasures of sensory detail, such as "camellia white lovely thighs, / lips whose softness melds like dew, / whose tongue is ever strange and new."

Even as he ponders characters such as the television icons of his childhood, the Lone Ranger and Tonto, for example, Cummins anticipates the real-world complexities that will become apparent soon enough, figured in his early consciousness as "the Shadow who knew evils that lurked in [the hearts of] men."

Cummins explored timeless themes of poetry and ponders artistic sensitivity as blessing or burden, offering homage to Shakespeare and W.C. Williams, Hart Crane, Ezra Pound, and Dylan Thomas. Invoking beloved fictional figures such as Don Quixote, Cummins poses questions that probe nostalgia, such as:

> Whom shall we consider the ultimate fool?
> Those who never stray beyond accepted rules
> Or the errant Don venturing from peak to cave
> Embracing life with craziness and with grace?

Alongside testaments to a life well lived are poems of moral and mortal reckoning, witnessing both epic tragedies and personal losses. And in these lyric ruminations Cummins offers one plausible response, with resonant humanity, to moral ambiguity and irreconcilable complexity, as in "Vietnam Redux: Three Photographs from the American War." Re-examining atrocities of that war, Cummins asks haunting questions: "Does agony ever atrophy? / Do terror and loss abate?" In poems graphic and unforgettable, his pointed commentary examines "our witness—our engagement—our collusion."

Invoking the searing image of Kim Phuc, "naked, / fleeing along the dirt road, / her soundless cry, / her scorched flesh," Cummins, with pointed double-entendre, "renders our conviction."

And yet, even with his profound awareness of the sometimes tragic consequences of human nature, Cummins argues the claim made by W.C. Williams: "We do not live in a sonnet world," and works to create a conscious haven: "Let's choose our sonnets... As we embrace romance, our sweet reality— / Here's to love, our poems and our posterity."

Kristin Herbert

CONTENTS

Newer Poems: 2012–2017

From *Under Cover*: Poems 2002–2011

From *A Postcard from Bali:* Poems 1966–2001

Newer Poems

2012–2017

CONTENTS

Newer Poems: 2012–2017

Awake to the subtle gesture, the almost unseen sign that beauty remains in our world, or will be born again to protest the inhuman trajectory the world has taken, these poems were written with the quiet clarity of a man who has offered his loving attention for more than seven decades, and a willingness to put his shoulder to the wheel. Many of the poems are triggered by the long, love and wonder he has found in "love's recall," as he has written. All of them seek to "fix truth beyond boundaries" as the poet places his gentle disposition against life's rigor, and even cruelty, as he continues his search for the places where tenderness, compassion and connection will be found.

Peter Levitt

The 9th Inning
for Ken

"Even when it's over it's not over."
                 — Charles Bernstein*

Yeah. We probably are heading into the 9th inning—
But there is this to say about the 9th inning:
Nellie Fox once fouled off 16 pitches
         in one at-bat,
USC came back in the college world series
         Down 7-0 and scored 8 to win;
some pitchers take a deliberately long time
            between pitches and some of their tosses
            take forever to reach the plate
            and some superstar hitters
            step out of the box incessantly
            before finishing their at-bat.
Somewhere in the twilight of his days
            a daydreaming hitter is still waiting
            for that Hoyt Wilhelm pitch to arrive,
            time of no concern to either.
Time thus postponed and as Rolfe** said,
            "Time is of the essence."
One at-bat can take a long time—
            3 and 2, with foul after foul,
            and then a free pass,
            no one out yet.

The manager may stroll out and jaw
        with the pitcher, maybe buying
        time for the reliever to get warm.
The reliever may amble in from the bullpen
        not charging out like Gagne
        but strolling in like Mariano—
        "Time is of the essence."
The umpire may inspect this or that ball,
        the game may be rain-delayed,
        the tarps rolled out and later
        rolled in while time is held in abeyance,
As sage Yogi said: "it ain't over 'til it's over"
        and the fat lady is sitting on her ass.

Remember too there is no clock in this game.
Sometimes games go into extra innings
        and no one ever knows
        when this might happen.
So 9th innings can stretch out—which is, isn't it,
        what we are all trying to do anyway?
Stretching it out like Joe D. going from 1st to 3rd
        (never once thrown out at 3rd),
stretching it out without looking backwards,
        for as Satchel once said,
        "the bastards may be gaining on you."
Stretching it out, loving every moment,
        living life as the gift it is—"time,"
        of course, "is of the essence."

A Hotel Lobby's Treasure Trove

A gift from my old college roomie—
An autographed baseball from the 1950 Yankees.
The names barely visible,
      Some faded beyond recognition,
The metaphor here too obvious to develop.
But names that are clear enough
      Excite me beyond reason.

These names may not mean much
To most readers, but to me
      Gene Woodling, Hank Bauer, Tommy Heinrich
Are magical talismans summoning
      Memories of more simple,
      Innocent days when trim green grass and
      The sound of a Louisville Slugger's wood
      Sending a cork-centered Spaulding ball
      Into flight was all-absorbing.
It was not about money,
      Who has your team bought and sold
      For next year's line-up;
It was a cast of characters you stayed with
      You knew them and their history
These guys were points of reference and stability
In your life, and being a fan was almost sacrosanct.

My roomie gathered these signatures in a hotel lobby—
      Not only was Joe D. there
      But Red Sox brother Dominick as well—

On the ball their names next to Vic Raschi, and, yes,
>> Just barely legible
>> With a magnifying glass
>> Phil Rizzuto too, wow!
And Eddie Lopat, Gil McDougald, and Mick Mantle
>> (Yes, he signed it "Mick")

So much, you see, depends upon these names,
Like abracadabra, embodying magic,
And if you don't understand that,
Either you weren't there, or even if you were
You really weren't; you missed it.
Look, there is Enos Country Slaughter and Dr. Bobby Brown,
No, not nicknames but denotations.
And yes, the skipper, Casey Stengel there, too.
So how could I not almost wet my pants
When my roomie sent me this ball?

September Song: Turning Eighty
(9-9-37)

Oh what the hell, let's give it a shot.
I tried evasion last year by writing
A rather ineffective, perhaps too cutesy
"Turning" poem—"On Turning Seventy-Nine."

So here it is, the milestone eighty—
Not itself any more peak or bleak
Than other numbers, nonetheless a harsh
Reminder of the "days that dwindle down."

Some poems of this ilk list key incidents,
Lasering in on births, deaths, loves, losses,
Citing highs and lows, lessons maybe learned,
And then, maybe not, thus to be repeated.
So if not these broad strokes, what then?
Well, I think I know. It came to me
Early this morning walking Mo Joe,
As always wagging his tail at life.

My turning eighty, I believe, needs to be
A wagging of my tales offered to whomever
Chooses to listen or is trapped in an audience
Obliged thereby to consider these words.

Recently a friend asked, "So, are you going
To write a depressing passage-of-time poem,
Such as sometimes, no, as oftentimes

Has been your wont?" "No," I say,
Just a simple grateful-for-my-being poem:
For being conscious of my precious few days,
For being capable of giving and receiving love,
For marriage and family and friends.

For forty years, and then forty more
Actually, Mo Joe and I realized this morning
That, beginning in Fort Wayne, Indiana, 1942,
I have been going to school for 75 years.
                              [without missing a year]
Am I not the happy scholar of my life?
With almost every golden day of said 75
Spent looking forward to each and every morning
To what those days promised to provide.

And the force igniting each day's light?
Simply promises supplied by hope,
Hope that somehow this poem, that novel,
This project, that encounter, might engender

Not only hope within others, but a respect
For reason, a love of ideas arrayed in brilliant
Images, visions clothed in silky flowing words,
From one glimpse of beauty and truth to the next.

Hope that someday the magnificence and mystery
Of the universe will awaken our species
To our common follies, our shared inheritance
And our precarious journey through unknown vastness.

Yes, hope and gratitude—a volume with eighty chapters.
A blink in cosmic time; my eternity on earth.
Hope and gratitude—the inheritance of a man
Blessed with a childhood of love and security—

Receiving gifts of unconditional parental love,
A supportive, adoring sister, attending strange schools
Which, as the leaves turned to flame, allowed space
And leisure to dabble, daydream and digress.
Later, an educator myself, blessed with employers
And fellow employees for whom risk-taking
Became, in retrospect, an unspoken given.
Responding always to the new with "Yes."

And a wild wife blessing me with children
Two acquired, two sired, all adored;
Then grandsons and granddaughters—
Our miraculous payback to posterity.
Yes, it all melts into air, into thin air,
Meanwhile, from the astonishment of birth
To the intrusion of death there is still—
à la Ulysses—much to seek and much to find.

But hold on, upfront I promised not
To wax depressive or dirge-like;
So let's stop here—allowing me to give thanks
And welcome the remaining time I'll spend with you.

A Lonely Sestet in Search Of

There are no beasts driving me into darkness,
No leopards nor lions nor she-wolves baring fangs,
No, it is the darkness itself that dominates
Stashing the very light away into caves;
And since we know dark will say the final say,
I have come to loathe the close of each day.
Night, unable to offer the elixir of sleep,
Presides over the dashing of restful dreams.
But now, at the turn, with only six lines
To counteract this octet's despotic designs,
We need to walk hand in hand with leniency,
Finding solace not in creeds but in the primacy
Of kindness, kindness which by its grace alone
Provides us modest means to meander home.

HCE: A Son-Not (?)

"Along the riverrun, past Eve and Adam's"

Zen I arouse wan fineheights mourning,
the dawn as false as Falstaff's filches,
et steamed thot evrivertebrate choired hear,
end soar, I lofted Hell's curtain eturnitee;
off coarse, wheez warrant awakt yet,
quantumely, the petals stile wear wrapt
white as haze-brake's cognizant bequest:
fore goddess stakes, wot in the whorl's awash?

Well, haven's conversayshun ensanguined thou/ought,
theirto, bye jimmeny, jollity and I rejoyced,
all mythos aside, we reprieved reality's alife,
no bridges available to reverse us in verse,
neverlessthee, love's for sail: here comes eternally.

It's a Guy Thing
—For M.C. Ford

Gilmore Field. Not there any more.
Now a mall with every sort of store
there where Triple-A heroes used to roam—
no more Carlos Bernier stealing home,
no more Fat Frankie Kelleher Dingers,
now Starbucks, Victoria's Secret, Macy's,
no more exhibitions with the Yankees—
just bookstore bios of Yogi and Mickey.

I met a friend recently and we two
began summoning names: Max West, Jack Graham,
guys I hadn't thought of for decades,
while my wife observed, utterly amazed;
on we obsessed: remember Luscious Luke Easter?
Remember Steve Bilko? Chuck Connors? Remember?

Straight and Loopy True

You can't be off the wall without a wall—
Any Fool will tell you the straight man
Must be as brilliant as the star, creating a reality
The star then deranges through his bizarre—
The straight man inflates the balloon,
The lead guy explodes it.

Groucho needed Margaret Dumont's imperviousness
To his outrageous insults to keep firing them off,
Her oblivious giving free rein to his wit,
Lou Costello required Abbott's indifference
To his peculiar predicaments
To provoke his over-the-top tantrums.

Quixote's enchantments endearing and sad
Seen through Sancho's loyal naïveté;
Hal only becomes king when Falstaff's
Sacrifices enhance his better half.
"Your money or your life!" The patented Benny pause,
"I'm thinking, I'm thinking"—who's the straight man here?

And Edgar Bergen, outlasting them all,
Playing a straight-man ventriloquist
To the tuxedo-clad wooden dummy he birthed
And bequeathed his brilliant, bratty humor;
Yessir, Charlie McCarthy answered every
Interview question Edgar Bergen was ever asked.

Perhaps we need become our own straight man—
Leading ourselves to where the crookèd lies,
Showing us the only way we become free
By understanding why it matters so
To know "Who's on first? Who? Yes,"
To tune in to what is loopy true.

Tell Me, Please?

"I was thinking," Alice said very politely,
"which is the best way out of this wood:
it's getting dark, would you tell me, please?"
                    —Lewis Carroll

Midway through these lovely, dark, and literary woods,
I pause, seeking to gain, as they say, my bearings,
and, honestly, to regain a sense of balance,
for while I may have reached the forest midway,
still I am nearing the end of my allotted stay,
and though the end does not seem imminent yet,
purchasing this pause and reflecting I think wise
as darkness descends and thickets sting the eyes.

Pausing, though, is not without its perils—
Rorschach-like the trees take on star-crossed lines
and images I can decipher only with smarting eyes;
it is, alas, as Emily observes, all too poignant,
all too impossible to fathom here on earth.
I surmise, Miss Alice, there may be no best way out.

Requests

For Richard Grayson (March 25, 1941–July 3, 2016)

I

"Play 'Die Walküre' as a tango"
"Play 'Für Elise' as if Stravinsky"
"Play the 'Pink Panther' and 'James Bond' themes
as if a Bach double fugue."

Patiently he would jot down requests,
ruminate for a moment,
shuffle his note cards,
peruse the keyboard
and then sally forth.

While we devotees attending his annual concert,
some for over thirty years, expressed delight,
never tiring of his magic, recognizing a few
tricks and patterns but still enjoying
enough surprises to keep us coming back.

II

When the cancer assailed him, and worsened,
when he, then we, knew
his life now in diminuendo
he handled it with the same
patience and grace as was his way.

At his bedside, the end now near,
an adoring colleague spoke to him

not knowing if he could hear
her expressions of love and admiration,

Suddenly she exclaimed, "Give me an 'A'."
He opened his eyes slightly and from deep
inside, gave her a gravelly, low-pitched "A,"
not flat, not sharp, clearly an "A".

Flies on the Pie

The indignities multiply
like flies on a pie,
a couple at first—
tingling in the toes,
numbness in the feet
as if a bunched-up sock,
then bitter news,
prostate cancer, "not"
the doctor informs,
"not the good kind—aggressive,"
so we go after it aggressively:
hormone alteration, radiation,
endless blood tests,
more flies on the pie,
soon sciatica joins the parade
first the right side, then
listing to the left—
discomfort now continual,
sleep positions challenged...
more flies, next,
a cataract, and a doctor
picks up anemia, more flies.
Oh yes, hearing loss too—
But I still love the pie,
shoo fly, shoo fly.

Remembering the Future

"It's a poor sort of memory that works only backwards,"
the queen remarked.

—Lewis Carroll

"When I use a word," Humpty Dumpty said,
"It means just what I choose it to mean,
nothing more, nothing less," which applies
to memory too, would you not agree?

That is to say, a given memory means
what we determine it to mean,
truth being not the issue,
nor probably even retrievable,
preserving persona the heart of the matter.

What memory selects to fasten upon
alone is memory's truth, embellished
through countless tellings, each polishing,
erasing residual qualms here and there,

memory being our private vault
safeguarding all the stories we require
to mollify our mirror each morning:
for within memory our selfhood abides,
within memory our future lies.

Which Is It?

Words
      hang around the psychic lounge,
loiterers looking
      to cadge an image,
phrases counter spinning
      round and round
like the little white ball
      roaming the roulette wheel,
hoping perchance
      to land on an apt metaphor
that will cash in
      hours of prospecting.
So.which is it—
      the vision or the parlance?
Which is it—
      the wish or the well?

What's in a Name?

Call me Paul. Though if
I had been misnamed Ishmael
or Saul would I have evolved
precisely as Paul? If Saul
peered into a mirror today, would he
see Paul staring back with incredulity?

I was called, I believe, to be Paul.
You see, my father so wrapped his ways
around the name, it had to be mine too.
Despite circularity, it became my certainty.

And though he died four decades ago,
I know his marrow mentors my bones,
His daffy dreams, eccentric sweetness withal,
What the hell else could I be but Paul?

A Summer Stroll

Poetry set forth on a stroll one day
inviting melody to accompany.
Driven by her destiny, melody agreed.

Then they recruited rhyme—a suave valet
to chime in, whenever, along the way,
thereby adding decorum to their soirée.

Next imagery was asked to describe
how she viewed this summer's day ;
she offered "serene as orchids on display."

Imagery also proposed they enlist meter
to help quicken their stylistic pace,
forging patterns into lilting rhythmic grace.

Thus as our entourage advanced
more compatriots fell into line
enlivening the procession with talents sublime,

to wit: metaphor was assigned to oversee
the tenor and taste of each conceit,
as if catering an elegant high tea.

Gradually they all came to embrace
Form, who, while sometimes quite strict,
nevertheless arranged a loose triadic shape.

Finally, poetry invited song to unify
the entire team—meter, metaphor and rhyme,
imagery, melody, form—all pleased to comply.

"So has a poem transpired?" a passer-by inquired.
"Well," song intoned, "hitherto this page was blank;
now look closely and tell us what you think."

"Wait," theme intervened, a newcomer to the scene,
"we have, so far, a nice mix of techniques,
but without me, we lack meaning and mystique!"

"True, perhaps," poetry replied, "but for now
I think it may suffice to avow
the act of crafting itself is the show."

Words, Words, Words

Just before eliding into sleep
it came to me last night,
whence? No matter, what came,
the notion that one uttered word
may summon a particular poet,
e.g., try "Usura," Ezra, of course,
or say "Brillig," "Gyre," "Rage, rage".
No, this isn't a quiz, just
a realization that given words
become so imbedded in given poems
that the word calls forth the poem.

Bravo, I say to these archers
whose words arrow their way
so deeply into our psyches.
Here a few more to entertain:
"Ravished, Promises, Debauchee"
or try "loaf, ice cream, spindrift";
Do they not recall Keats,
Frost, and Dickinson?
Walt, Wallace, and Hart Crane?
These single words keys to kingdoms
awaiting oddballs like you and me.

A Stalker

On occasion I sense a poem stalking me,
soft whispers as from a dimly recalled dream
hinting at revelations just beyond reach,
stranding me, unable to close the breach;
misleading as by a seasoned striptease artist
offering disguises which provoke false arrests,
thus imprisoning all metaphors and images
while dispatching vision off to storage.

How may I contact this aloof voice?
Perhaps retreating to a place where noise
can find no purchase, where leisure reigns,
allowing dreams to gain their own terrain,
where urgent lines like vines upon a trellis
attain that light which honors earthly promise.

show up

you have a cold, are feeling run down, so you make a last-min-ute excuse and you don't attend the dinner where you would have met the woman with whom you would have designed a new school when you were offered the job to do so and not knowing her would mean you didn't get her recommendation for a music teacher whom you would have interviewed, hired, fallen in love with, and married and designed innovative music programs with and housed overseas students in your home and traveled to Bora Bora and the Galapagos with and she would not have introduced you to the man with whom you traveled to Vienna and China and whose biography you would write, and you wouldn't have acquired two step-daughters and two step-grandsons and you wouldn't have had the two daughters you and the woman you would not have met have had together and you would not have had the three grandchildren they have brought into the world and your world and so on and so on and had you let your cold and feeling run-down trigger your last-minute excuse and non-atten-dance, you wouldn't be here now writing this and you would not know where you would be . . . .

Yesterday is Another Day

Did he, truly, by then
      "not give a damn"
striding out into the transient mist
      of a vanishing mirage?

And why, eight decades hence,
      do we embrace their misfortune,
as Gable, a.k.a. Captain Butler, departs
      fed up with valiant fantasies?

Or see Deborah Kerr and Donna Reed
      evacuating shortly after Pearl Harbor,
leaving behind their lost loves—
      Montgomery dead, Burt an army lifer;

they sail away and, complying with legend,
      toss their leis into the sea;
if the leis float back to shore,
      "You will return someday..."
Yet we know the currents
      will pay them little heed;
we know these two will not return,
      their losses for eternity.

Or see Alan Ladd riding away
      through distant gravestones on Boot Hill
in yet another scenario
      of the hero receding into history

While Brandon, a.k.a. Joey, chases after him
      imploring: "Shane, come back!"
But we know that he cannot;
      nor can we.

EndsandBeginsand

"Poor old Michael Finnegan, begin again..."

Whilst sleeking screenarios wi' prognoses
of changés that seam witless in retro spectre,
wee inherent not so vary mulch,
nor ring down any lurking certains, nore
stave any wave, for votz knot to unlearn
when lessons lessen, lesser, and less?
wan as fin said agin, its awl their
"for whole the world to see," nes pas?
wot time begat, we've besot, lost,
re-searched, besmirched, and while mean,
the hole lot's wound down and, yea,
nonminded, so watt's on earth to sea
that ain't jest an anti sea dense? well,
ile be damned if envy of oz no...

A Ghostly Waltz

I.

I find myself staring
        across the studio;
for forty-three years now:
        her focus, always,
in the moment,
        riveted upon her students—
this one's glissandos feathering
        across the keys.

II.

Passage after restless passage
        exquisitely nuanced,
fragmented episodes which she,
        like a sorceress
has drawn out of him,
        his "la valse" exposing
undercurrents of a lost world,
        unveiling the death and decay
of the danse macabre coda,
        a scene that he
at seventeen, should not
        have been able to grasp.

III.

Yet there in his playing
        nostalgia devolving to the ominous
as she guides his descent
        into shadows of an old elegance
embracing Ravel's apotheosis
        of the ghostly Viennese waltz.

IV.

And all the while
        I witness the show
in pride, in amazement,
        a warming in my loins
summoning me back
        to an earlier era.

Sunny Side Up

—for Avani Rose Colella Cummins
born August 3, 2012

"Sunny side up," the pediatrician
proclaimed, pulling back the curtain
of your mother's belly, and there,

there you were, staring up,
making your debut upon the stage
of this magical, fractured world,

staring into the bright lights.
May you stay sunny side up,
night or day, whatever the play.

Sweet Prince

"Good night, sweet prince,
And flights of angels sing thee to thy rest"
Hamlet, Act V, Scene ii

To know him was to respect him.
Can there be a more grand tribute?
Somehow his quiet kindness, listening,
Truly listening, not just waiting for
An opportunity to intrude, listening
With interest and responsiveness
And thus encouraging the rest of us
To be who we are, to reveal
A bit more about ourselves because we
Trusted him, trusted ourselves with him.

The Lakers, the Warriors, opera, the current political scene,
The economy, the law, whatever the domain,
His clear intelligence shed light
And we all, without fully realizing it,
Sought his ideas and felt not fully informed
Until we knew his take—yet that take
Was never imposed on a discussion or
A debate—it was simply, if you want
An insight or two before going off with
Half-baked ideas, then let's discuss.

I particularly treasure the evenings spent
Listening to operas, coupled with his

Explanations of why this tenor,
That soprano was so magnificent.
I know my yardstick for great
Performances is rooted in his influences:
Ferrier's Micaela, Leontyne's Butterfly,
Leonard Warren's Forza and Biotto's libretti.
I had always hoped he would write
Biotto's biography—it was his dream.

Mostly, though, I will miss his quiet dignity.
His love of all of us seemingly limitless
Yet rarely judgmental; and did I mention
Humor? Well, a sense of humor both earthy
And existential. From Tom Lehrer and Lenny Bruce
To Laurel and Hardy and Chaplin to Harold Lloyd
And on to more recent comics, his laughter
For me, contagious as well as enlightening
And always with a grace that transcends self—
An awareness of irony and mystery.

A dear friend recently told me, "I cannot
Imagine this world without you" and I,
I cannot imagine this world without Ken.
I adored my sister and was twice blessed
When she married Ken, and thrice when he
Married Ann. The world without Ken
Will be diminished for so many of us.
He was our Prince, our friend, our rock.
We will now have to ask ourselves, over
And over again, when in need,
What would Ken say?

In memory of Kenneth Coogan Adams
November 18, 1928–September 12, 2017

Under Cover

2002–2011

From *Under Cover*: Poems 2002–2011

Paul's poetry bespeaks his concern about life in all its manifestations: his family, his community, the larger world, and especially the students for whom he has created so many energized schools all offering every child what he wishes for his own. Paul's poetry points to equal justice, points away from war, violence and greed. His great love and reverence for language, his keen eye for detail and, yes, his appreciation for humor all enliven his poetry, which in its power might actually call into being a better, more equitable world. His is a life steeped in poetry, in layers of meaning and allusion. He writes as he lives - for his life, for the lives of all of us. His poetry and his work are one, the same. No difference between them.

Ann Colburn
May 2018

Under Cover

The skies were pretty much blue those years,
Quiet streets lined with burnished maple trees,
The horizon lay where it was supposed to be
Ever so far away wherein vision disappears;
Neighborhoods welcomed carts with ice-cream chimes,
And fireflies designed galaxies spread above the ground
As random owls floated inquiries over cricket rounds,
And we listened spellbound while summoned to bedtime.
Lights out, I listened under the covers to Jack Benny,
To The Shadow who knew evils that lurked in men,
The Lone Ranger and Tonto triumphing again and again,
To the reassuring deference of Rochester, Amos and Andy.
All was quite well ordered, quite a set of certainties—
It seemed that all was as it was ordained to be.

The Aura of Love

How do they know where they must go?
The leatherback turtle, the ancient albatross,
The petrels and sooty shearwaters,
journeying thousands of miles
across oceans and over continents
following some intricate mysterious compass.

How is it that two sojourners
venturing forth on two remote paths
find their ways to create one voyage?
He from Italy to Iceland to New Orleans,
she Barcelona to Monterey and back to L.A.,
separately seeking to rescue the wilds
from civilized chaos, yet, improbably
they meet, and to many this may seem
rather clear evidence of destiny;

Each determined to live in integrity
amidst our crumbling structures of vanity,
each determined to meet aggressive ignorance
with truth and passion their only shield.
We witness this new union in surprise,
inspired as if a wild rain
had cleaned the air and brightened the skies;
what is more, the aura of their love
delights those of us drawn into their circle.

From the tops of trees to plastic seas,

from the Pacific gyre to Burning Man,
from the L.A. River to the Mississippi
From Vancouver to Tijuana,
from dinosaur bones to tango violin,
from desert storm sculptures to organic gardens,
wherever their quixotic sallying may lead,
they are at home in each other's presence
and we are blessed to formalize that home.

Bailey: A Golden Retriever

He loves retrieving balls,
That's his DNA and he
Would retrieve all day,
All night until he dropped
If you would keep throwing;
But that's not what defines him—
Any more than the affection
He craves and would receive
In endless tummy-rubs
As long as you would rub;
But that too is not defining—
Nor the tail-thumping if you
So much as look his way or say
His name, if ever so softly,
Soft, soft thump;
But that as well does not define.
No, it is his eyes—
A trace of sadness programmed perhaps
To say creatures like me are rare
And this world does not grasp
The essence of why we are here;
Eyes which combine wild and tame
In a sweetness so pure
That he fills the void;
And playing catch,
Tummy-rubbing and tail-thumping
Compel us to look into the world
Which lies behind his gentle eyes.

Mo Joe

Sometimes he comes to me
with two,
sometimes only one,
sometimes three—
tennis balls in his mouth;
not an easy feat.
One is simple,
true, two—more complicated,
requiring flexible jowls,
but three, that's something
and he knows it is,
wriggling his rear
like a pole dancer,
his tail flapping
like a windshield wiper,
smiling at his own
achievement.
Yes, smiling, they do—
Goldens smile—ask any vet,
he or she will tell you,
Goldens smile
and Moe Joe—
that's his name—
smiles when he pulls off
a "three-fer":
So let's give credit
where credit is due.

Joseph and His Sons

How could he have been
         my father's father?
He as simple as
         Des Moines summer rain;
his son fired by dreams
         more wild than winter wind;
he given to scripture and rhymed homilies
         made real by practice;
his son embracing the Alger myth
         made real by endless striving;
he an Iowa postal clerk
         reliable as sunrise;
his son a hustler, entrepreneur,
         unpredictable as ambition;
he selecting a dime for me
         from his coin purse;
his son displaying
         a million-dollar bank loan;
their bond, their basis of relating
         still to me a mystery.
But this I know, Joseph,
         my father's father,
sometimes you appear in evening quiet
         like a ghostly lullaby,
making your sweet spirit known
         as on the day you died,
the only time in my life
         I ever saw my father cry.

"We Do Not Live in a Sonnet World"
—W.C. Williams

Says who, my lovely, my bonnie lass mate?
Let's choose our sonnets and brilliant blue bonnets.
In form and informally plighting our troths and estates,
for whither we are is now and forever our billet;
and the conjugate lives we craft no more daft
than refining beats to set a line in time,
this sonnet-seeking need, like magic or witchcraft,
our daily fare learning how and why to recombine.
Though some dismiss such amorous themes and tropes
as obsolete, passé, and prone to mere display,
and while free verse may roam the markets unopposed,
two lives may find their rhymes in loving play.
As we embrace romance, our sweet reality—
here's to love, our poems, and our posterity.

On Hearing George Shearing

Do we not hunger for perfection?
Though each may have our point-to-proof,
our operational definition of such,
for me an embodiment materialized at eleven,
my sister shepherding me into a cocktail lounge
in New York City, hiding in a back corner booth
so I could imbibe sweet melodies wafting
out from the piano, the muse wearing sunglasses
creating perfection, each chord progression,
each riff, each pause, each harmony
played, I now believe, the way God,
if God could, would play the piano.
Each decade of my life I have made
pilgrimages to his public offerings
hearing from those black and white rows
a series of Platonic revelations,
with nary a false move,
never anything but pure grace.

Spirals

Made so fairly well
With delicate spire and whorl.
—Tennyson, "Maud"

I

Curving around and around as they do
receding from or approaching a fixed
point, turning upon whatever axis,
coiling as if in their own whirlpool,
spirals navigate a destined course
dictated by whatever their form—
from footballs to galaxies.
They may bind notebooks,
define airplane maneuvers,
economics, turbines or gears,
implying how so much coheres.

II

Spirals at first were as elusive
as measuring the curves of Archimedes,
yet my father persevered in teaching me—
"let the ball slide off and float out"
and frequently it floated fairly well:
some would wobble in the wind,
some he called "dying quails,"

but some, by God, some spiraled,
and then we both smiled.
Older, I tried gripping the laces
but strangely this didn't feel right, so
I threw without fingering the laces,
and lo, spirals came in clusters
and became my mojo.

III

During my high school career
mostly spirals were hurled forth
to find my friend Terry's hands,
soft as a retriever's jowls;
or to Long John Holloway,
slow of foot but sticky-fingered;
or to the fleet, galloping Cliff
with hands so stiff you had to
feather it to him exactly. One time
he forgot to look back and,
some forty yards downfield, the ball
descended into his outstretched hands perfectly,
nestling there while he sped
like a waiter offering fans a loaf of bread,
sprinting into the end zone afraid
to alter his bearing lest he break the spell.

IV

Spirals then were to me as sensual

as holding dark-eyed Nancy's delicate hand
at the Friday night picture show.
And to this very day,
some six decades away,
I enjoy an occasional reprise,
and spirals still engender smiles.

After Laura

"She used to let her golden hair fly free,"
or so I see in simple yesterdays
where love's first stirrings staged their plays
in scenes of sweet erotic fantasies;
as under one enchanted laurel tree
my Aphrodite set me so ablaze
I scarcely knew the summer nights from days
while lost in amatory reveries;
and though strict time tempers youthful Eros
as the mundane adamantly marches forth
tamping down the flowering of romance,
graciously golden hair will reappear, luminous,
and, like free-flowing wind from the north,
stir my heart, summoning us to dance.

First line of Petrarch's Sonnet 69, translated by
Thomas G. Bergin
(*Crofts Classics*, 1966).

Tossing Hair

She tosses back long black hair
A conductor-like sweep of the hand
Prefacing careful considerations with this
Gesture unconsciously graceful as waves
Of the tall Kansas grass
Wafting in the summer winds;
Stirring and rearranging the gravity
In our conference rooms and seminars,
Her gesture almost cloying in its cadences
Yet changing the very currents of our thought.
When her hair began to disappear,
She adorned rainbows of scarves
Then soon allowed us to see
A new silver-gray crop of hair,
A terrible new beauty born there
And we could feel a shift
In the weight of the air.

1937

A random foray, a stray antique store wall pin-up calendar displaying brown long hair, red lips open wide, white teeth. But what caught my eye—the date: Nineteen thirty-seven—my birth year. And lo, at the bottom, my month—September, oh, the days dwindle down indeed. While my mother was giving me life on this day the ninth, a Japanese air raid killed three hundred Chinese refugees, four days before my mother's father died, four days after Thomas Masaryk too, and two weeks beyond him Bessie Smith. FDR began the year saying "I see one-third of a nation ill-housed, ill-clad, ill-nourished." Mao and Chiang began separation woes The agonies of war came to us in April not from Pathé News but a painting, etching in our collective consciousness the evisceration of souls in Guernica. Exiled in Mexico, Trotsky implored for the overthrow of Stalin. Random headlines outline more of the times: Hindenburg Blows Up, Dow Chemical Begins Manufacturing Plastic, Hollywood Favorite Jean Harlow Dies, Somoza Becomes President of Nicaragua, Louis Defeats Braddock, Earhart Lost at Sea, Disney Produces "Snow White," Buchenwald Established: Fourth Camp. And if you watch the Louis-Braddock reels in the corner of the screen as Louis's arm is being raised you will see a ghostly figure slip into view, turn Braddock over and photograph his dazed face—the figure is my father, the photo lost in a family move. So 1937 ended with these: Maurice Ravel Dies, Jane Fonda is Born, Java Man Linked with Homo Sapiens—Java Man, it seems, may have been the victim of brain-feasting headhunters, and Japan begins atrocities in Nanking as my lovely mother held me in her arms.

Vietnam Redux: Three Photographs from the American War

Prelude: Evidence

Some images scald the heart
more than electric shock
staying not just during pain
but as long as consciousness remains.
To illustrate: consider these
whose click defined a war—
haunting still decades afar,
three photographs inadvertently
exposing a tragic beginning,
an atavistic middle,
the inevitable end.

One: Protestation (1964)

Motionless, perfectly still in lotus pose,
sitting in his own immolation pyre,
frozen in engulfing flames
this monk assumes a people's pain,
his Buddha flesh testifying in prophetic fire,
on behalf of the world that should be
where life would be allowed to live.

Two: Summary Judgment (1968)

An execution—
not after a trial,
not in an institution,
almost casually,
General Nguyen (Neoc Loan)
holds the pistol in his hand and
there on the street, the man's
hands bound behind his back,
his head just begins its contorted
explosion, the pistol, bullet, and impact
all captured in that grotesque blast,
a life shattered before our eyes,
our witness—our engagement—our collusion.

Three: Indictment (June 8, 1972)

Kim Phuc, naked
fleeing along the dirt road,
her soundless cry,
her scorched flesh,
her agony palpable.
From the skies
a rainstorm of napalm
burns indiscriminately
whatever it touches,
Soldiers, children, trees,
this little girl
renders our conviction.

Postscript: Sentencing (2009)

Does agony ever atrophy?
Do terror and loss abate?
Are these pictures mere relics
of entertaining evening news
captured in stills then simply shelved
in archives and out-of-print books?

Who can say?
Millions erased.
The monk's ashes
floating upon moonlit lily ponds,
executed soldiers now footnotes
in statistical directories.
Lessons learned?
Two more wars since,
conflict everywhere on earth.
The girl in the picture?
She survived, clothes
cover her scars.
Now in Canada,
she lives simply.

Forgiveness her compass.
Perhaps though secretly
Wearing a vestige of pride
Knowing she exposed evil
stopped a war.

Three Rivers: The North Fork

Sometimes the idea of a place transcends
the place itself, or is it that the idea engenders
a passion in your heart for the place?
Say our getaway in foothills beyond the city,
a small home along the tree-canopied river,
the river rush a sort of seasonal symphony,
an idea of family planted firmly in this retreat
with ongoing projects—this garden, that fire pit,
this apple orchard along the north property line,
that wraparound deck, this river-rock wall,
each project a step toward capturing a dream
of designing a generational gathering site,
the ritual of building together a sort of shrine
to quiet, to meals, to holding whatever
each believes to be the essence of reverence,
of revering each other, our time together,
of revering the simple blessings of being,
each act of reverence enhanced by the place,
by the idea of creating our uncommon setting,
this place extending in each mind to the very
limits of mortality with intimations of beyond.

The Simple Science of Wealth

First you must conflate your initial strategy
into new and highly attractive formulas
and wrap them into an emerging complexity
for successful apportions to be reconfigured
by conveying the package into more intricate systems
via destinations unevident and indistinct
and reassigned through differentiated rearrangements,
then sell positions in these myriad transactions
to buyers thrice removed from fluctuating prices
earlier determined by acknowledged masters of design
who wrap their figures into new complexities
and immediately transfer the derivations
into unique and more attractive formulations
of successful reapportionments to be reconfigured
for new destinations uncharted and distinct
through new buyers who repackage the outgrowths
into modified and highly intriguing recalculations
immediately reassigned through diversified systems
for successful and more attractive reformulations
wherein everyone engaged accumulates immense profits.

The Cranes of Bosque del Apache
—For Bill and Patrick

Ghosting down in gray pointillistic swaths
From out of the silver sunset sky
Myriad spirals in skein after skein alight
Upon the shallow bronze marshy ponds;
Primeval sandhill cranes and raucous snow geese
Intuiting refuge from predators natural and otherwise.
With our magnified eyes we pay homage
To their ancient rituals, knowing deep inside
That their endangerment endangers us all.

We return at dawn, a final pilgrimage
To witness their frenzied ascent into day,
Applauding with a wing-flapping roar
Like the surf pounding the shore,
The snow geese in wild disarray
Outlining the sky in tumultuous circles.
Their shrieking clamor quickens our blood
In a scene of such exquisite bedlam.

They settle once before another go
As though offering a rehearsal
Before the next heart-dizzying show.
Meanwhile the stately cranes begin
To unfold their light sectional steps
As if testing the water with a toe
Before completing the gesture.

A couple of hops and they lift,
Tubular vessels with midway wings
Assuming their prehistoric pose,
As they have for fifty thousand years.

Eyes

I have seen this look before
The grave recognition, the eyes
Fixing truth beyond boundaries,
Beyond instruments of the temporal
Beyond all charts, drips,
Scans, tubes, tests, zigzag needles
Moving across the screens
Like Dow-Jones quotations.
Still the eyes show and tell,
Saying to me, her brother,
I know now I am dying.
Eyes that see horizons dimming,
Space no longer expanding,
Hope flickering like candles in a draft.
Humor now an artifice to help
Others with little to laugh of.
Our decades have devolved to this,
Grasped by shared histories,
Soon to mist into ether,
Staring into each other's eyes.

The Huddle and The Grand Hotel

I.

I had not noticed until the other day
that the two prints on my study wall
are siblings—one a hotel, the other
an architectural rendering of a restaurant,
my father's return to the coffee-shop stage
two decades after his undergrad debut.
The same name, The Huddle, in revival,
its sign now comprising six separate stick-
poles each floating a mosaic letter—
H.U.D.D.L.E. in colored rectangular blocks,
tossed up in the air like a deck of cards;
this giant object marquee grabbing the eye,
yet also displayed on vinyl menu covers.

II.

It was the Fifties and my dad was there
pioneering with Bob's Big Boy and the Googies
folks,
the Huddle his dream of doing it right—
combining design, décor, food, ambiance,
in buildings with good taste or, from one critic,
"we need buildings that taste good"—
this my father's grasp of a futuristic
fashion later ennobled as a school—
a reach for his Utopian landscape.

III.

Meanwhile, hanging next to my Huddle rendering,
a framed facsimile of the Grand Hotel,
our vacation halfway stop on Mackinac Island
ferried in our family Pontiac into upper Michigan.
The stately hotel constructed of lovely white pine,
offering its glorious view of the island's round lighthouse
while surveying the shimmering white-capped lake.

IV.

The slender classical columns wrapped
around the world's largest colonial porch
at this, the world's largest summer hotel—
etching into the memory of my sister and me
a lifelong image of Edenic majesty,
that place, as things were then,
we would often imagine revisiting,
oh, to be skipping down the long wide porch
looking out at the vast cobalt-blue water,
the fluffy white clouds our someday pillows,
what could be more grand?

V.

What then do I interpret there upon my wall,
the Huddle and the Grand Hotel? Only this—
my father's tomorrows, his children's yesterdays,

his Utopia, our Arcadia, blend in the time,
merge in dreams of what was, what seems
what might have been, and what in fact has been.
Thus it is, you see, these meals of memories served
by the Huddle and at the Grand Hotel
Taste so awfully good.

Saved

It started out as a Jimmy
Stewart mowing the lawn
And June Allyson smiling over
The picket fence kind of scene.
Whistling songs by Sammy Cahn—
"Put them in a box, tie 'em with a ribbon,"
When a Joan Crawford sort of cloud
Passed overhead and a dark
Richard Widmark-like sedan approached
And the sky was no longer Doris Day
But almost a black dahlia night
Right then as the two Edward G. guys
In trenchcoats debarked and slouched
Towards the erstwhile Frank Capra driveway
Now transformed into a Cagney alley,
I saw I was in a Hitchcock jam
And needed a John Wayne-like rescue,
When salvation came as a Shane-type
Guy who was quicker with the trigger
Than Jack Wilson—who was himself fast,
Fast, Joey, "He was fast on the draw,"
But my guy was better and I woke up,
Alive, ready to meet reality,
Ready to be, say, Atticus Finch.

Junior High: Ode to Donny

He was certainly strange
And we didn't understand
Often arriving with milk residue
Curdled on his upper lip
Like a leftover ring in the sink;
But unlike current TV ads—
Stars glamorizing milk
With thin white lines
Mustaching sensual lips—
His display incited ridicule.
In time some guys learned
That sustained taunting
Provoked him to near hysteria—
Soon a common sideshow at recess:
We laughed and he frothed.
No adults told us anything.
Then one day he was gone.
Decades later I read Mailer's
Why Are We in Vietnam?
It wasn't about the war at all
Just about men hunting in Alaska,
Once torturing a wounded bear.
Why the title, I wondered?
An image surfaced,
I saw white-lipped Donny.
I remembered how we circled him
And laughed.

Thanatos Unleashed

Preface

They have sown the wind
and they shall reap the whirlwind.
—Hosea 8:7

One sky changed the skies forever.
Never will a clear sky be seen
Without that hint of fiery figures
Emerging from the earth like an effigy;
Forever the skies outlined in mushrooms
Rising each from each—no pure clouds
Ever again—white skies in ruins forever.

Part I: August

Nagasaki is now a dead city.
(Japanese news agency, shortly after the city was bombed)

If just a few contiguous clouds had parted,
The explosion of fire would have burst
Upon other children skipping off to school,
Other blue-suited commuters hurrying to work,
Other housewives watering their morning glories,
Removing their breakfast tea and cakes.
These were blessed by the weather—
Not targeted earlier for the fire-bombing

And now spared by capricious clouds,
These people of Kokura went about life.
Not so at nearby Nagasaki.

The bomb must be dropped.
Complicitly a few clouds parted:
"There, there is a target,
Pull the lever,
Drop the bomb."
The bomb must be dropped.
Sweeney banked the Bock's Car
Rising into a lesser history,
Number two, not as illustrious,
Fewer indexes in texts,
Fewer journal entries, novels, documentaries.
August 9: Three days behind.

Part II: The Fat Man
Those scientists who dropped the atomic bomb,
what did they think would happen if they dropped it?
  —Japanese schoolgirl survivor

A meteor in reverse
Erupted from the earth,
A giant totem,
A pillar of fire
Sprouting a daemonic mushroom.
Then surrealistic replicas
As the Fat Man sallied

Into the Urakami Valley.

Later black rain began to fall,
Showering its poison
Upon roasted souls breathing their last,
Upon broken spines, shattered skeletons,
Black rain laying a palette
Of ink upon forms of decomposing flesh.

Schoolchildren incinerated in an instant.
Dead carp burned white, floating
Upside down in irradiated streams;
Everywhere searing into souls of the living,
Everywhere searing, the screams.

Part III: Three Days Before

A scientist said to his father,
"Science has now known sin,"
And do you know what his father said?
He said, "What is sin?"
—Kurt Vonnegut, *Cat's Cradle*

Three days before, Shigeyoshi Morimoto
Was in Hiroshima, making anti-aircraft kites,
Miraculously he survived.
He intuited another fireball over his city,
Hurried back home, arriving just at 11:00 A.M.;
He was telling his wife of the blinding blue flash

At the very moment their city died, too.
Again Morimoto survived.
Not so for Dr. Tsuneo
Who hurried home on August six.
Resting at Nagasaki medical College,
He died with half the personnel in a blink.
The others tried to flee the inferno,
In vain. Then the black rain began to fall.

Part IV: Captain Beahan's Birthday

Bomb away.
—Captain Kermit Beahan

"Bombs Away," Bombardier Beahan said,
Then quickly revised: "Bomb Away."
As Bock's Car lurched upward,
Self separation timing switches opened.
Barometric pressure closed other switches
As Fat Man fell toward an outdoor stadium
On shaded banks of the Urakami River.
Radar switches activated,
Arming and firing levers closed,
The shining black projectile neared the earth.
A few curious witnesses saw it fall just
As detonators triggered the conflagration.
At the medical college Doctor Shirabe
Could hear the agony of patients
Trapped in their floating coffins as he stumbled

To higher ground behind the ashery.
Bock's Car was followed by a second plane
The Great Artiste could see only a fireball
Rising toward them, a cloud from Hades.
Below them, later in the afternoon,
Remnants of the medical college staff
Gathered on a hillside attending the dying.
No more screams echoed in the pyres below,
the city a graveyard without tombstones,
Kikuo Fukahori staggered home to find
It was destroyed, crushing his five children.
His wife, alive, stared at him utterly dazed,
"Her tongue protruding from a swollen, blistering face."
Kevin Beahan went to bed exhausted;
It was his twenty-seventh birthday.
Some of the crew had trouble sleeping.

Part V: Afterward

There is nothing one man will not do to another.
—Carolyn Forché

Once a year a few may remember—
Speeches, memorials, tributes here and there,
Morimoto, Tsuneo, Fukahori, Shirabe,
Randomly invoked, most likely not.
Meanwhile ashes float and settle all over Earth.
Histories defend Little Boy and Fat Man:

Regrettable necessities to save lives.
Thousands vaporized without a trace.
Few tangibles remain beyond the fading
Echoes of scorched screams in forgotten shades.
But what I want to know,
Is it possible
        To re-imagine the unimaginable?
Is it possible
        To ever find just utterance?
Is memory truly an adequate bulwark
        Against repetition, against finality?
And are there limits to what we do
        To each other?

"A Sort of Pilgrim"

Coole Park is, to be sure, a beautiful meadow,
though no more so than many others, or so
until an Irish poet became inspired to see
and retrieve words for the grace he perceived.
And so I went there once to celebrate
the poet's take on the beauty of that place;
in fact, my visit was mostly a pilgrimage
to absorb his brilliant, sacred images.
That July the meadow dry, brown, and silent,
there were no wild swans floating by, yet
happily, I must confess, I saw them rise,
whereupon I was quite overcome with surprise.
Tears filled my eyes and quickened my heart;
indeed, I saw the ghostly swans of Coole Park.

The Bridge

A place becomes a place
Because of what you bring there
And also what you leave behind.
An ordinary bridge, for example,
Becomes a conduit from mundane
Realms to where wishes reign
All transformed by childhood dreams;
It can be the link between three
Pairs of sisters, two on the west side
And one on the east, who cross
By foot, skate, and tricycle
And later venture underneath,
Risking trolls and unknown shapes,
Then journey up the watercress creek
Knapsacks tied neatly on sticks
With peanut butter and jelly rations
(Once one of them brought the Bible)
Six little girls seeking secret lairs
To share revelations of fleeting days.
Under the bridge also useful at dusk
To hide awaiting that climactic instant
To streak in and kick the can
Freeing teammates from bondage.
The bridge a perfect location
For neighborhood photos, especially one
With five of the six, sitting on the rail
(The sixth off somewhere else)
In this photo—(ages four to six) they sit

Making their faces look funny,
Each secure in who she was.

o   o   o

More than a decade later
They reassemble, assuming the old poses
Making their beautiful young women's faces
Funny again as they delight in time,
In continuity, in each other,
Celebrating themselves in passage,
Affirming both sides of the bridge,
More aware now of the shadows below.

A Postcard from Bali
1966–2001

Cummins has spent the last 30 years developing his pedagogical ideas through various schools he has founded. And throughout all this, his steady companion, poetry, has provided ballast for his imagination, philosophies that resonate, a salve for grief, and finally language to explain experience, or as he says, "language trying to get at the heart of the matter."

Libby Motika

From *A Postcard from Bali:* Poems 1966–2001

A Postcard from Bali

Jon
decades have passed
and memories still surface
like dolphins breaching for air
I never wrote to your dad
he's probably dead now
mine is
I wanted to ask him for a picture
but you were gone
and that was that
i got the news in grad school
wandered Brattle Street
drifted into a bar
poured down a few unhelpful beers
and returned to dinner
there was no one to talk to

you changed me
I remember meeting
in line freshman year
skinny, long neck, carrot hair
you asked me what I was reading
hell, Jon, I didn't read then
I was dumb as dough
but you gave me *Catcher*
selecting my first books
with a parent's care
you set me in motion

your prodding, ridicule
angered me into learning
so while you
Baudelaire in your hip pocket
dropped out, hopped a freighter
and traveled the world
I began to read
to learn about the written world
that world you knew so well
yet feared to join
i still read like a psalm
your postcard from Bali
the content long since memorized
now time has changed
the calendar, useful only
to mark off children's birthdays
somehow for me
you are still a postcard away

i say your name and there you are
harassing me
determined to make a silk purse

when your body broke on the Big Sur rocks
was some muse released who gravitates
to jazz records with Kid Ory, George Lewis,
Louis Armstrong and all the Creole crew?
or when someone with tragic sense picks up Unamuno
are you there applauding over his shoulder?
there were only a few who knew you

do we hold exclusive power to call
and spirit you back?

I dream, Jon, of two motorcycle rides
you and I, high,
flying through the Palo Alto countryside,
turning over, tumbling down the hill
ass over teakettle laughing
we were as close as wafer and wine
i can't pretend any premonitions
we simply said goodbye the next day
i never thought it would end there
when you and your bike were flying again
hurtling through the cold wind
to the rocks below
was it an accident, Jon?
while i think i know
i see a picture in slow motion reverse
see you tumbling back up the hill
laughing your way back.

The Pilgrim's Way
—for Anna

Make no mistake—
You don't make
A journey
For sake
Of a destination.
You go
Where you go
To find out
Why you are there.
The cold wind
And fevers,
The steep climbs,
The solitude,
Squinting heat,
The doubts
Are not simply
Errant adventures
To recount later
As fireside stories;
They are immediate
Pieces of discovery
Of you.
Cervantes may have been
Cruel to Quixote,
No matter, the Don
Designed himself,
Willed what he became.

No, you go
Where you go
To define the extent
Of you.

Puma on a Leash

They say that the brain
Stores it all like a vault
Preserving every image,
That all is retrievable if only
The right combination
Can be discovered.
While that may be, it seems to me
That most images simply disappear,
While others stick like peanut butter
To the roof of your mouth, their savor
Persisting beyond the initial taste.
This is how it is with me
And my children, the youngest,
For example, I see in my mind's eye
Flying down the driveway, her three
Wheeler's oversized tires reverberating,
Youngest of the neighborhood kids,
Eyes wild with excitement;
Or the time in Yosemite, resisting
Entreaties to jump into the rapids slide
Down the smooth rocks to the pool below,
The water at summer's early high
From a winter surfeit of snow, a play
Paradise but terrifying to a seven-year-old.
All day she held back but at dusk,
As we packed to walk up the trail,
She strode to the river and jumped—
She simply could not leave without

Doing what everyone else had done;
Or in eighth grade soccer, the goalie,
Taking a direct shot in the face
Downed, zap, like a Joe Louis foe,
We all raced to where she lay
Traces of blood trickling through her braces.
Eyes closed for a five or six count, then
Leaping to her feet and running back
To her goalie's den to stand guard.
The crowd standing there, stunned,
As she gave her message: "No whining
Little girl crap for me—let's get on."
Or two years later, different sport,
Her first championship game
Getting the game-winning hit
Enlivened to be at bat
With the game at stake.
Lately this gift image from abroad:
Traveling by herself throughout Bolivia,
Pausing for two weeks to volunteer
In a rain forest animal shelter.
Her job: to exercise the puma.
Somehow this image fits the bill—
Emily running along a jungle trail
With a puma on a leash.

Scenic Vietnam

I heard a radio ad,
a week or so ago,
to visit "scenic Vietnam"
(three syllables, not two
as LBJ was wont to do).
A stunning ad,
I should think—
"Scenic Vietnam."
So what would we see?
Would we see ash gardens
of the immolated monks?
The burnished bones
from My Lai?
A polished gash in the earth
emblazoned with the names
of two million or so
Vietnamese souls?
Would the best, brightest
agencies
arrange for us to see
an orange hue, here, there
in the paddy cavities?
In the barren trees?

Here, there, everywhere...
Would we see the stone age
as promised by Lemay?
Lights at the end of tunnels?

Would we see deserted farms
and ghostly forest catacombs?
Would we visit a portrait museum
of the heroes we financed—Ky, Diem,
Ngo Dinh Nhu, Madame Nhu, Thieu?
Would we be escorted
from featured city to city
say—Da Nang, Hue, An Khe?
Cities destroyed though saved?
Would we be encouraged
to crawl through the rat
tunnels underneath napalm carpets
laid by the U.S. of A.?
If so, then let us go,
You and me and Uncle Sam,
to the truly scenic Vietnam.

Dinner with Kurahashi

There in the elegant restaurant,
customary gifts already exchanged,
amidst the chardonnay and crème brulée,
the conversation turned, and Mr. Kurahashi
placed his cloth napkin to his face
and then, he sobbed, his body wracked
with tears of the moment, tears of the ages.
He told us of his earliest memories:
born in nineteen forty-two,
bringing a lunch box to the dock—
a two-year-old saying goodbye
to his brilliant father—
honors student,
young engineer,
now an emperor's soldier,
sent away to glorify an abstraction;
he assailed the upside-down world of war—
of daylight turned into night
and the daylight of the nights:
propaganda dense as a thousand cranes
shadowing the noon sky,
raining down from B-29s;
he recalled the thick, black midnight pitch
of Kyoto's blacked-out sky
ignited in white yellow wild light,
the distant firestorms from Osaka.
He told us of learning that his father,
the soldier with the lunch box, died

somewhere, anonymously in the Philippines,
lost to his only son forever.
Who could know this soldier's dying thoughts,
lying there in the torpid tropical air,
silence his only accompanist.
Still, tonight he is in loving company.

Free Fall in Barcelona
—for Liesl

The tiny antiquarian curio store,
dusty, dimly lit. A tourist perusing things,
I stepped behind a table in the rear—
an uncovered basement lay a step away.
Suddenly, I plunged into darkness,
a free fall into terror,
time suspended by a factor of impending death:
was this magical realism when waking dreams
tyrannize three-dimensional time
surprising a chosen few for a round trip
to relate what mysteries lie beyond the abyss
of styx and stone crypts, to be Lazarus
to my family or anyone else who would listen?
Would I discover what lies beyond the pitch-
black silence of sound and sense of self?
Might I find my father in fathoms below
to ask: do you, the dead, know us in any way;
is there any bridge beyond love and mortality?
Or was this a fall into the eternal void
of inflationary time and ever-expanding space?
Just simply a journey of no return—
an absurd departure with no forgiveness,
no farewells, no expressions of abiding love?
Perhaps answers lay poised in the spectral gloom
but cement hard as a headstone
abruptly stopped my descent
and detonated all speculation.

Instead, what I found was the storekeeper
standing over me, aghast,
fear choking his voice
asking me could I move?
Though utterly stunned, I ran a few quick tests:
flex fingers, wiggle toes, turn head and neck:
and then it was clear what I needed to do:
I must stand up;
I must reassure him I was okay, and that,
together, we should climb up the ladder
out of the uncovered basement.

Sidewalks

Standing under a street light
bent like Harold Lloyd's clock,
it is better generally to move
than to purchase alternatives;
meanwhile shadows linger on cracked sidewalks
as in silent midnight dreams.
"Hallelujah!" the crazy screams
painting furiously an invisible canvas.
And there, by god, there emerges
our doppelganger the ragpicker
standing within the mute canvas,
his hands searching empty pockets,
eyes staring at a statue of god
in the lonely center square.

Shirley

In the dark alley, narrow, remote,
no streetlights to be seen,
no doorhandles on the doors,
yet as natural as childbirth
a door opened and hands reached out,
gently, firmly gathering the boy inside,
the room warm and pungent with presences,
a chorus of hands undressing,
wrapping him in dream-soft sheets
on an altar-like bed,
covering his passive naked body
in tongued caresses and kisses.

Years later sitting alone in darkness—
a candlelight evensong, broken light
rising to the ceiling like spider webs
riding the currents of summer wind,
a hand touched my shoulder,
a scent of lotion surprising me,
a sudden invitation from the shadows
summoning me from my hiding place,
and like a moth curving to the light
I was led into a courtyard
of moonless silence,
her warm moist hand enclosing mine,
her smile terrifying—
she knew what there is to know
and I knew that I did not.

Her fingers lightly traced my face,
"May I walk with you?"
and I dimly nodded "yes".
Later she placed my hands
in places they had never been,
her hand inviting me.
She touched me and I became,
like a sculptor shaping first clay.

A Benediction

I dialed my father in this dream,
Though deceased for fifteen years,
There he was on the phone:

A wistful voice sweet and lonely
Sifting seemingly through air
From his sphere to mine.

I told him I was fine
And that I missed him dearly;
"That's nice, son," he said.

It seemed clear indeed
That he was preoccupied
Though pleased to hear from me

That being dead did not allow
Him to know or say too much—
Perhaps it is just too sad to know.

And yet the voice also seemed to say
"It's all okay, son," we had love
And love does not go away.

Fourth Quarter Shadows: 1954

Late November dusk descended
>Shadows moving up the field
>>But we were not.

Two minutes to go,
>We're down a touchdown
>>Last game of the year.

Suddenly coach calls for Terry and me,
>We're juniors, best friends,
>>He sends us in.

"Throw it," coach tells me,
>I'm a Q.B, Terry's an end.
>>And the shadows are moving on

Then all those Saturdays and summers
>Practicing patterns with my dad,
>>Begin to pay off.

We get hot—post, buttonhook, slant, down and out,
>One, two, three, four
>>Completions in a row,

Up the darkening field we go,
>It never occurs to me
>>To throw to anyone else.
We're really moving now,

Only one minute to go
        But I know Terry and I can...

Except that the coach—
        Inexplicably, just as we reach
            The shadows of their goal posts—

Pulls us out and puts
        The senior Q.B. and end back in.
            Terry and I are stunned.

And then our drive
        Grinds to a halt.
            We lose.

Later the coach explains: "I had to,
        They're my seniors;
            It was their last game."

Nevertheless, he allows,
        "You guys put on quite a show,"
            The shadows now cover the field.

But, of course,
        I know in retrospect
            What we would have done—

"Terry," I would say in the huddle,
        The guys viewing me now
            With a new confidence,

"You throw a fake block

        At the right corner D.B., fall, roll,

                Come up and fade to the right

Back corner of the end zone

        Like we practiced last summer

                With my dad.

I'll fake a half-back dive,

        And roll out naked

                To the right,

I'll find you."

        That's what memory affirms

                What surely would have been.

Of course, we would have won.

        But that was 46 years ago,

                Terry died last year. Dad's gone too.

And why the hell am I

        Thinking now, so clearly, of then?

                And the shadows move on.

Red Rover

Red Rover, Red Rover
Send Emily over
Send Emily over
And over again.
And over and over
Red Rover, Red Rover
And over and over
And over again.

And as she grows older
Red Rover, Red Rover
Still she comes over
And over again.
And over and over
Red Rover, Red Rover
And over and over
And over again.

But then comes a day
When is becomes was
And was then has been
Oh Rover, Red Rover
And over and over
Is over, is over.
It's over, Red Rover,
It's over again.

Overlooking Jena: 1939
(For Herbert)

Here we were
surrounded by a forest.
There were even trees
      inside the walls.
Between the kitchen
      and laundry
stood the Goethe Oak.
      Its inscription:
"Above all the treetops
      there is peace."
Yet as though they knew
this was no place for them—
      there were no birds,
         not a one
     in Buchenwald.

A Gentleman from Iowa

When I think of my grandfather,
Dead now for decades,
I think first of fine white hair—
As thick as August wheat,
As pure as starlight,
As soft as dandelion dust;
I think of notebooks of homilies
Filled with a lifetime of cut-outs
Of the "Do unto others" variety;
But mostly I think of one afternoon:
My father and I, summoned
By his plaintive calls for help,
From different ends of the hall,
We arrived at his bathroom
And found him wedged between
The toilet and the wall.
Unable to move, with a twinkle
In his lovely peaceful eyes,
He said not a word but let
The situation speak for itself.
There was no embarrassment,
Simply light laughter and love,
A recognition from three generations
Of what has been, what will come,
And what holds it all together.

Flying to Philadelphia

High above these fields of clouds
I dream of you girls, boarding
your team bus, armed with gum
your panoply packed: bats and mitts,
a sponge for one sprained palm,
balm, rubber cleats, ice packs
to crack and apply after slides
batting gloves, helmets, knee pads,
may they protect you from all harm;
If only I could be your pads
absorbing every scrape, each defeat,
it will not be. The rule:
give and then recede.
Hours and hours of pitch and hit,
retrieving ground balls on fields
all degree of smooth and rough,
before dinner rituals of catch,
each year your throws more secure
bringing me the sting of celebration.
Now both of you, beautiful in uniform,
testing yourself in the game.
Give and then recede.
The leaves are singing green,
the sky cloudless and clear,
spring air is crisp and clean,
go to bat, my loves, and swing.

Hegel Shooting Baskets in the Garden

For years these weeds entangled their court:
"You never help in my garden."
"You never shoot baskets with me."
And it was true—they never did.
And though the jump shots nicely bloomed
And daisies and impatiens grew,
Silence guarded them one on one.
Yet she began in time to see
Netted twine in baskets of wisteria vine
And swishing of the ball sensual as a petal fall:
Conversely he soon came to feel
The glory of the morning peonies
In an apotheosis of summer roses.
Driving, pressing, laying in beds of hyacinths
Pushing up and pushing down,
Scents of jasmine blooming in the night,
Their pollinated thighs entwined as birds of Paradise.
Now they play in floral fields of basketballs
Applauded by laurel leaves and petal falls.

Nina

Through loud cocktail smoke
she first appears,
a tray balancing on her fingers
like a leaf on rapids
as she glides through lonely men
gazing at her lush sensual thighs,
her peach-light, smooth white skin,
her smile sweet as jasmine.
My heart quickens,
touched by something less than lust,
something strangely paternal
and I ask for her name.
"Nina," she says,
pronouncing the "i" as in "die",
a hint of the old South.
I give her my address—
"if you're ever in L.A."
The jazz band breaks into
"Oh When the Saints"...
Several months later she calls
"I'm here in town," she says.
We get together.
The first morning after
I awake startled, feeling the warm
dampness of the sheets.
"Sometimes," she confesses
"I wet my bed."
Soon the midnight calls:

"I'll kill myself if you don't come"
and I would come, barely awake,
would rock her to sleep;
then months of counseling,
we enroll her in adult classes.

For a time she is thrilled,
glimpsing this world of words,
she admires Blanche Dubois.
Still she wets her bed.
After a year or more,
I resign.
She moves from pad to pad,
calling at times for help,
then she leaves town.

Ten years or so later
I receive a letter
from upstate New York,
with pictures of her and husband,
her face round as puff pastry,
her tiny frame now wide
as is his.
"We are happy," she says,
"we drink too much,
we laugh a lot,
we go to movie shows.
I don't wet my bed any more.
How are you?"

Sonnet: A Husband in Waiting

Sometimes I stand in the bedroom shadows arrested
While she, naked, arranges her wet, light brown hair,
Beads of water glisten like dawn on her breasts
And though I have seen this before, still I stare:
Perhaps it is the powder whiteness of her thighs
Which holds my eyes as if I were hypnotized.
And though her arms are summer soft and loose,
No longer sculpture smooth as twenty years ago,
Yet all is cast lovely in the bathroom glare—
Three dozen lights framing a marquee mirror
As if she were the star of my secret show,
Even now ever more familiar, more sensual
And spying there from my silent station withal
I feel applause gathering in my thighs
And once again am taken quite by surprise.

Hallowe'en 1977
—For Anna

Lined up on a stage,
of a makeshift outdoor sort,
five hideous witches and demons
faced the enraptured audience
to strike terror
in whosoever should dare observe;
the judge—a Hollywood actor/director—
awarded four consolation prizes before
giving a verbal drumroll to present
his grand prize to the ultimate fiend,
and, placing his hands over its head,
removed the mask of this monster
of the rustic canyon park.
Almost expressionless, moon faced, cherubic,
her cheeks white and soft as love,
an almost smile the antonym of her mask,
my eyes moistened forever—
for I had seen the face of God.

Icarus

High above the sea I was free
As I climbed higher and higher
Tears washed my eyes
The ancient winds lashed my face
Crete slowly shrinking to a seed
Petals of the sun began unfolding
One by one into an orange-red orifice
Inviting me in and so I climbed
Arose and sought to meld my very soul
Within the burning brilliance
And Oh, the melodies, my father,
A surprise of a thousand melodies
Harmonizing with cries of ecstasy
All the lyres of the heavens
Arising to a glissando of fire.

I heard your voice
Urging me to return
To go no farther
But how could I stop?
Everything you taught me
Compelled me to proceed
The stories we would read
Daily lessons of success
Stories of all that you achieved,
How could I return?
You were at my back.
Must I not take your design

And push it on?
Oh, Father, architect of my youth
I wished to give you full measure
Of what you gave to me
And as I fell to the sea
My body glistening with heat
Scalding me with melting wax
Still I could not wait to return
To tell you of the sun's burning
A burning inside my heart.
It was our journey I made.
The wings were yours.

Four Worlds

Perhaps the muse was lost
or knocked slightly off course
from her celestial flights
spilling her magic dust
upon the sleeping little girl
in the sleepy Midwest town,
Wisconsin daughter of two
Bavarian immigrants—one
a simple brewery worker
the other fumbling her rosary
whenever her son played football.
Finding the one person in town
who could feed her soul,
she studied piano with the imperative
by which a moth is drawn to light.

Now fifty years beyond
she too is a piano teacher.
Still struck by the muse,
she sprinkles her own dust
on unsuspecting children.
Each day they come and go,
their parents as unaware
of the transfigurations
as hers once were.
You might mistake the scene
for some ordinary fare:
a neighborhood piano teacher

replete with gold stars and licorice
bestowed for a well turned piece,
but you would be mistaken
for here three worlds
are preserved and transferred
to those with chosen ears to hear.
Here Shenker, Schnabel, Tzerko
haunt little souls who do not
know who these ghosts were in life;
but their fire, passion, and urgings
are present as she digs deeply
into this phrase, caresses that motif.

With those who strive and care
her lessons are timeless—
lost to the passage of daily time
they slave over a measure—
three against two, four against five—
she cannot get anywhere on time,
yet in these meticulous dots, circles,
staves, tadpole designs and the like
she is as precise as an astral engineer.
The lessons are wild and loud—
footstamping, clapping, shouting, singing,
exaggerated crashings on the two keyboards—
once she bellowed at a Chinese boy
that he "played like a wooden Indian";
he was, of course, baffled, but now
he doesn't play that way anymore.

The lessons sometimes begin at seven
and end beyond midnight as owls
whoo approval of the show.
from Shenker she learned to go
beyond recipe to a rapprochement
between theory and the composer's thought;
from Schnabel to see mysteries
hidden between the lines and spaces;
from Tzerko that absolutely nothing
less than passion will ever do.
These worlds the children
chance upon when entering her studio.

Linda

One day in late Fall
When time was child slow
I stayed after school
Alone in the library
Reading of a lost crow
Searching for his mate;
And when I wandered home at dusk
Lost in the lost bird's woes,
I saw a girl from my school
There across the street.
She did not see me
Hiding in the willow blind shade
Staring, watching her move by
A sylph of darkening night
Long brown hair loose as wind
Washing over her bare shoulders
Like sea grass in slow tides.
I could feel a strange warming
Of surprised limbs
As the street lights began to ignite,
One at a time,
Could feel my temple tighten
While the inaugural evening owl glided by.
I closed my eyes dizzy with this new
And barely found my way home.

Crossing the River

To get to the other side
Is difficult
The water is swift
The rocks are slippery
And they are spaced
Irregularly
You must reach one foot out
Tentatively
And then anchor it
As securely as
Possible
Then carefully set the rear foot
Forward to the tiny dry spot
You see on the next rock
Soon you will get the feel
Of this procedure but
This all is leading
To the one place in the river
Where the irregularity
Is wider than anywhere before
Where a tentative reach
Won't work
Where security is not
Possible
Where you either turn
Back
Or you
Jump.

Advice

Oh Father, my Father, Oh what must I do?
They're burning our streets and beating me blue.
"Listen, my son, I'll tell you the truth:
Get a close haircut and spit-shine your shoes."

Oh Mother, my Mother, my confusions remove,
I long to embrace her whose hair is so smooth.
"Now listen, my son, although you're confused,
Cut your hair close and spit-shine your shoes."

Oh Teacher, my Teacher, your life with me share,
What books ought I read? What thoughts do I dare?
"Oh Student, my Student, of dissent you beware.
Shine those dull shoes and cut short your hair."

Oh Preacher, my Preacher, does God really care?
Are all races equal? Are laws just and fair?
"Boy—here's the answer, no need to despair:
Shine those new shoes and cut short that hair."

Awakenings

("History is a nightmare from which I am trying to awake.")
—James Joyce

"To hell with it,"
the Sorcerer said,
took out his blade
and opened up a major vein
letting in an exquisite
wild wind—
an ocean-rending,
mountain-moving,
tree-snapping
wild wind.
Out of the earth's gash
the soldiers gushed,
tyrants flushed
in rivers of their
own blood.
While winds extinguished
all the folderol of war:
borders blurred,
idols split,
flags frayed
scattering in the whirl.
And when the wind withdrew
it was as though
the Cosmos held its breath.
The ocean lay still,
a crease in the silent sky

allowing threads of light
to warm the shores
where sand and sea combine
to make one plain.
See the dolphins celebrate
in artful figure eights.

Author Bio

Paul Cummins is an educator, writer and social entrepreneur. From Stanford (BA) to Harvard (M.A.T) to USC (PhD) to classroom teaching, 1960 - 1971 to founding and co-founding six schools including private schools such as Crossroads School and Tree Academy and Public Charter Schools such as Camino Nuevo Charter School to founding outreach programs - P. S. Arts and The Coalition For Engaged Education. In all the ventures, he has been a champion for quality education , especially for at risk, foster and incarcerated youth.

His publications include an autobiography, 'Confessions Of A Headmaster', three other books on education, two children's books, four collections of essays, a biography of a holocaust survivor, 'Dachau Song' and with this book, three volumes of poetry.

Paul and his music teacher, co-educator wife, Mary Ann live in Santa Monica, California. They have four daughters, five grandchildren and many dreams for a better world.

CPSIA information can be obtained
at www.ICGtesting.com
Printed in the USA
LVHW090757181220
673927LV00011B/3/J

9 780999 845295